CATALINA

TILE

CATALINA
TILE

OF THE MAGIC ISLE

LEE ROSENTHAL

Edited by Lynn Downey

WINDGATE PRESS: SAUSALITO, CALIFORNIA

ACKNOWLEDGMENTS

I would like to express my gratitude to the following: Lynn Downey, writer and archivist, for putting together and making sense out of my notes; Patricia Moore, Director/Curator of the Santa Catalina Island Museum, for her many historical contributions and her unfailing moral support; Malcolm Renton, retired Vice President of the Santa Catalina Island Company, who answered my questions so many times and who gave me a perspective of the plant operation that no one else had; Joseph A. Taylor, President of Tile Heritage Foundation, for constantly sharing his knowledge of tile making and tile history with me and encouraging me over the rough spots; Kris Williamson, Vice President of the Santa Catalina Island Company, for doing what she can to preserve the old tiles; Donna Harrison of the Santa Catalina Island Company Planning Department for searching the company photo files for anything usable; Bernice Limbeck Gallant, Oliver Greenbaum, Earl Limbeck, Gloria Lopez, John Tyler, D.D.S., and Joe Saucedo, all former workers at the tile plant, for sharing their stories and information with me; Earl Hansen and Clarke Merrill for driving me around Avalon scouting out beautiful tile installations.

Collectors have been very generous in sharing their collections and allowing me to photograph them, especially Ray and Dorothy Beach, Allen and Laurie Carter, Mike Duff, Alex and Carolyn Dutzi, John Fletcher, Reed and Diane Glover, Mr. and Mrs. Mark Hoefs, Michael Kreil, Mr. and Mrs. Mike Marincovich, Patricia and Bill Meister, Ray and Jo Miller, Paul Neil, Will Richards, Jon Rippey, Mr. and Mrs. Ronald Rindge, Joe and Tina Voci. For finding room for me on many impromptu trips to the island, my very warmest thanks to my dear friends Raymond and Dorothy Beach, Patricia and Bruce Moore, Russ and Anna Neil, and Johnnie and Jean Windle. My thanks also to Richard Keit, Bill Lou, Richard Miller, Maria Poindexter, Dorothy Shepard, Dr. James Stifler and to my daughter Ann and her husband Michael Wolf who have been with me all the way. Without your contributions it wouldn't have happened.

Lee Rosenthal

PHOTOGRAPH ACKNOWLEDGEMENTS: All photographs are by Lee Rosenthal except for the following pages: Mike Duff – 53, 70. Richard Miller – 3, 5, 9, 10, 12, 15, 18, 20, 22, 25, 29, 38, 39, 41, 52, 54B, 54BL, 56, 57, 59, 65, 67, 68, and decorative tiles at top of text pages. The Tile Heritage Foundation, 2, 4, 21, 23B, 26T, 30, 31, 33, 40T, 42, 46, 47, 51, 58, 60, 76T.

Typography by Top Hat Typography, San Mateo, California

Copy Editor, Marian G. Witwer

Library of Congress Cataloging-in Publication Data
Catalina Tile of the Magic Isle
by Lee Rosenthal

    Includes Index.

    ISBN 0-915269-10-4

1. Catalina Tiles (Catalina, California) — History
2. Catalina Tiles — Description   3. Catalina Island
(Catalina, California) — History 4. Tile — Decoration
and ornament 5. Santa Catalina Island Company

This book is dedicated to John and Jean Windle

Back Cover Photograph: Lee Rosenthal

SECOND PRINTING
Printed in Korea by Sung In Printing America, Inc.

Designed by Linda Bonnett

Windgate Press   P.O. Box 1715   Sausalito, California 94966

CONTENTS

FOREWORD

AVALON! There is tile everywhere, a tile historian's dream come true. Walking the streets one can't help but marvel at the vibrant colors of the ceramic surfaces set between the lush greens of surrounding hills and the sparkling blues of the vast sea beyond. When I first visited Catalina in June of 1987, I heard talk of a woman and her daughter who had been wandering the island taking rubbings of the different tile surfaces. I thought to myself, "I'm not alone!" and I was right. Lee Rosenthal and I soon met, and now we serve together on the board of the Tile Heritage Foundation working to preserve ceramic surfaces across America.

Catalina tiles embody the *esprit* of their creator William Wrigley Jr. and reflect the vision of his son, Philip. Both were practical men who foresaw the economic and social benefits of a clay products operation enhancing the development of their picturesque island town. The fact that the raw materials were available locally was a fortuitous discovery. The Wrigleys were promoters striving to attract tourists to a then remote semi-tropical paradise, and decorative tiles lent themselves beautifully to this endeavor. Integrated into the Mediterranean-style architecture and often incorporating local themes, the tiles were distinctly patterned and colored in brilliant glazes, reflecting the area's romantic past.

Although similar in appearance to other tiles manufactured on the mainland, Catalina tiles were unique, not so much in design but in being so fully integrated into the culture of the island community. For those who came to visit, the tiles served as a visual enhancement of the island experience. Tiles, and later art pottery pieces, were taken home as souvenirs, reminders of the exotic paradise left behind.

Today, Catalina tiles are in danger. Although tourism remains an important part of the local economy, there is little official attention paid to the colorful ceramic surfaces that adorn the quaint streets of Avalon. These historic tiles are being threatened by indifference; one by one they are damaged, destroyed or removed.

Lee Rosenthal's book is a celebration of a colorful segment of our ceramic heritage, reflecting the aspirations of the many islanders involved. Today, the legacy is ours to share. Our hope is that with the increased knowledge of these unique clay objects, care will be taken to preserve what remains for the thousands more who will visit this magical island in the years to come.

Joseph A. Taylor

TILE HERITAGE FOUNDATION

Glass Bottom Boat at Seal Rocks, Catalina Island, California

C-3—Flying Fish, Santa Catalina, Calif.

CATALINA ISLAND CALIFORNIA
"The Magic Isle"

MISS CATALINA

THE BIRD PARK

THE CASINO

"Fairest Isle, All Isles Excelling"*

Santa Catalina Island, as the old song goes, lies "26 miles across the sea" from southern California, one of the links in the lovely chain known as the Channel Islands. Mt. Orizaba, the highest point on the 76-square-mile island, stands 2,125 feet above sea level; ravines and cliffs drop down to the many

9

*John Dryden, *King Arthur*, 1691

small coves scattered along its shore. The island's history is a complicated litany of explorers, otter hunters, smugglers, squatters, entrepreneurs and developers, all of whom left their marks.

Before its European discovery, Catalina was populated by Native Americans identified by anthropologists as Gabrielenos, though they called themselves Pimugnans. They lived at sites known today as Little Harbor, Avalon and Two Harbors. From the abundant soapstone on the island, they created cooking utensils, tools and ceremonial objects which they regularly traded with their neighbors on the mainland and the other Channel Islands. They built plank canoes considered to be among the finest of Native American vessels.

Santa Catalina Island is "discovered" every day by tourists and vacationers, but the first westerner to record his finding was navigator Juan Rodriguez Cabrillo, who called the island San Salvador and claimed it for Spain in 1542. Another sixty years went by before the island was "discovered" again. Explorer Sebastian Vizcaino sighted it in 1602 and once more claimed the island for King Philip III of Spain. Having spotted the island on November 24, the feast day of St. Catherine, he named it Santa Catalina in her honor. In 1769 the Portola expedition, making its way up the California coast, claimed Catalina for Spain for the third time.

The island was a lure for ship captains and fur trappers who discovered not only Catalina's harbors, but its large population of sea otters, whose pelts were greatly prized in China. Despite Spain's prohibition against foreign vessels engaging in trade and otter hunting in California, intrepid hunters managed to fill their vessels with pelts as the 18th century came to a close.

The first American ship to come to the island was the *Lelia Byrd* in 1805, commanded by William Shaler. He had been trading illegally along the coast and the previous year had exchanged shots with Spanish authorities in San Diego. When his ship needed repairs he chose the safe haven of Santa Catalina Island. American and Russian otter hunters and Yankee traders found the remote island an ideal base from which to launch their hunting and smuggling operations. When Mexico gained its independence from Spain in 1821, Santa Catalina Island, along with the rest of California, became a province of the new country. The Mexican government permitted trade but charged tariffs, so the island continued to be a base for smugglers. These men understandably left few written records, but those that have survived make no mention of the native islanders. It is probable that by this time the few remaining Native Americans who had not succumbed to European diseases to which they had little immunity had left the island to live at or around the Missions.

After the mid-nineteenth century, Catalina's chain of ownership became rather more complicated. Thomas Robbins, a naturalized Mexican who had been delivering mail by boat along the California coast, had petitioned for title to Catalina as early as

Crested Crane tile mural

1839. Governor Pio Pico granted the island to Robbins on July 4, 1846, just days before the Americans sailed into Monterey Bay. In 1850 Jose Maria Covarrubias bought the island from Robbins for $10,000, only to sell it to Santa Barbara lawyer Albert Packard in 1853 for the unlikely sum of $1,000. There was a brief gold rush fanned by rumors on the island in the 1860s. Some miners did find silver, not gold, but the cost of mining was prohibitive and by the mid-1860s the miners had nearly all left the island. Perhaps they didn't feel comfortable sharing the island with its other inhabitants at the time: the Union Army. Catalina was then under consideration as a reservation for "troublesome" northern California Indians and the Army built a barracks there to house the troops surveying the island's resources. The soldiers tolerated the presence of legitimate miners on the island, but after the Indian relocation plan was scrapped a year later the soldiers left. The barracks at Two Harbors is still standing and is still in use serving other purposes.

Between 1858 and 1867 portions of Catalina were sold to a variety of people. Between 1863 and 1867 eccentric millionaire James Lick, an astronomer for whom the Lick Observatory was later named, purchased all the separate portions for $23,000 each. At his death in 1876 his trustees were given title to the island that they sold to George R. Shatto in 1887 for $200,000. Shatto was the first to foresee Catalina's resort and development potential. He created and subdivided a town by the bay soon to be christened "Avalon." Shatto's sister-in-law is credited with choosing the name, taking it from Tennyson's *Idylls of the King.* Shatto drew up a plan for the city, laid out streets and auctioned off lots for a variety of prices depending on size and view. On the smaller lots summer visitors pitched tents or built lean-to shelters that they dismantled at the end of their holiday. For his wealthier guests Shatto built the Metropole Hotel. Steamers brought visitors from the mainland who swam, fished, and enjoyed the beaches and coves of the island.

Unfortunately, Shatto's dream was short-lived. Despite the island's popularity, he could not keep up the mortgage payments to the James Lick trustees and they eventually reclaimed the island. In 1892 Catalina was again sold, this time to William Banning, the son

Temporary and permanent residences, Avalon, c. 1890.

Avalon Bay, 1990.

Avalon Bay, 1898.

of Phineas Banning who had founded the town of Wilmington and developed stagecoach and steamer transportation in southern California. In 1896 the Banning family, three brothers and two sisters, formed a development enterprise called the Santa Catalina Island Company.

Under the Bannings' management, the town of Avalon grew and more people came to pitch their tents in the town and on the beaches. A stagecoach took visitors on tours of the interior valleys, and an incline railway was constructed to give a breathtaking view of Avalon Bay. By 1903 the *Lady Lou,* a glass-bottomed power boat, was showing visitors the beauty of the abundant marine life that inhabits the water around Avalon. Along with the tourists came more permanent settlers, who found the year-round life on the island much to their liking.

The Banning family made some permanent changes to the face of the island. In 1895, a tunnel was blasted through the large rock known as Sugarloaf Point between Avalon Bay and adjacent Descanso Bay to provide easy access to one of the three Banning homes. The tunnel collapsed in 1906, creating room for a coast road from what is now Casino Point to Descanso Bay and forming two rock formations out of one: Big Sugarloaf and Little Sugarloaf.

The year 1915 was heartbreaking for Catalina Islanders. On November 29 a disastrous fire raged through Avalon, leveling a third of the town. The Metropole Hotel was completely destroyed. In an attempt to recoup their losses, the Bannings built a new

Marlin plaque.

hotel, the St. Catherine at Descanso Bay, but none-theless they were soon forced to sell.

Ironically, all previous island owners and explorers had no idea that the very soil on which they walked had properties which would have provided them with much-needed building materials and the means to create objects of beauty. It was the island's new owner, legendary businessman William Wrigley, Jr., who found the island's secret.

Str. "Catalina"

Magic Charm of the "Enchanted Isle", Catalina, Calif.

AVALON AND BAY FROM THE CHIMES TOWER

Catalina ISLAND CALIFORNIA

FLYING FISH

COPYRIGHT MCMLI, BY CURT TEICH & CO., INC., CHICAGO, U.S.

THE WRIGLEY RESIDENCE ON MT. ADA, AVALON

The City of Avalon

Mr. Wrigley's Island

William Wrigley, Jr. was born in Philadelphia in 1861. He was eleven years old when he first left home and family to seek his fortune, but he returned a few weeks later. Expelled from school because of a prank, he was put to work in his father's soap factory. Tending the kettles wasn't very

satisfying, and he talked his parents into letting him become one of the salesmen. By the time he was twenty-four he had married Ada Foote, and at twenty-nine he was ready to move west. His father sent him to Chicago to open a branch of the family business with a cousin and one salesman. The competition was fierce; but when young William began giving "premiums" with purchases of soap and baking powder, business suddenly improved.

How Mr. Wrigley became interested in chewing gum is not certain, but in 1892 one could purchase a half pound of Wrigley baking powder for ten cents and receive two free packages of gum. Soon chewing gum was a much better seller than either soap or baking powder. By 1894 when his son Philip was born, William Wrigley, Jr. was in the chewing gum business to stay. From then on, his life resembled the all-American success story. He rode the waves of triumph and failure with the same energy, astonishing his colleagues, one of whom said, "I have never seen Mr. Wrigley worried. In crises that would have crushed many men, he remained calm and cheerful." Mr. Wrigley's acumen and enterprise were confirmed in 1932 when *Fortune* magazine published an extensive article about his life and career.[1]

Throughout the first decade of the 20th century he continued to thrive, building his fortune and making acquisitions which included the Chicago Cubs baseball team. Mr. and Mrs. Wrigley purchased a house in Pasadena to enjoy the mild California winters. In 1917 he persuaded the Chicago Cubs management to train the team in Pasadena that spring. By that time he had become a thorough southern California "booster."

While in Pasadena, Mr. Wrigley had purchased a small interest in the real estate firm of Blankenhorn and Hunter. In 1919 the company heard that the Bannings were selling Catalina Island. Mr. Wrigley was contacted by phone and asked if he would be interested in putting up enough money to help purchase the choice property. The island must have represented a new and exciting outlet for the businessman's inexhaustible energies, for he bought the major interest in the Santa Catalina Island Company, sight unseen.

Several weeks later Philip Wrigley, recently discharged from the Navy, accompanied his parents on their first trip to Catalina Island, where they stayed at the St. Catherine Hotel. The first morning after their arrival, Mrs. Ada Wrigley called her husband to the window—they were both early risers—and as they watched the sunrise she said, "I could live here forever." Mr. Wrigley felt the same, and by the end of 1919 he had bought out Blankenhorn and Hunter, becoming sole owner of Santa Catalina Island.

Asked by a Los Angeles reporter what he planned to do with his new acquisition, Mr. Wrigley replied:

□ While my motive in purchasing the island is largely a romantic one, I am going to leave no stone unturned to make it a refuge from worry and work for the rich and poor. Step by step, as business judgment dictates, and as the expert I shall put in charge advises, the buildings and other improvements will be constructed.[2]

Avalon school.

Tents at Island Villa Annex, c.1915.

The "expert" he was referring to was contractor David M. Renton, whom he had met in Pasadena. Mr. Renton had impressed him favorably at their first meeting, a story related by son Malcolm Renton in a note to me in 1992.

☐ It was Saturday. In those days most construction firms were closed, but my father was a very ambitious person and was still working at his lumber yard. Mr. Albert Conrad, who was Mr. Wrigley's landscape foreman, had tried to buy a small amount of lumber from a nearby yard but was told they were closed and to come back Monday. He went to my father's yard and my father gladly accommodated him. Later, when Mr. Wrigley wanted to have a Turkish steam bath installed in his residence, he asked Albert Conrad to suggest a good contractor. Mr. Conrad recommended my father. Other work followed and Mr. Wrigley was so pleased with the work and the promptness with which it was done that he persuaded my father to go with him on an inspection tour of the island.

On this first visit, Mr. Wrigley asked David Renton to give up his mainland business and to make his life's work the transformation of Avalon into a vacation paradise. He accepted the offer and was made general manager of all the construction work for the Santa Catalina Island Company.

The improvement campaign began immediately. New steamers were purchased to make the trip from the mainland more comfortable; the sewer system was updated, a power plant was constructed and a reservoir was built. The old tent colony was replaced by "bungalettes" with maid service: tidy, little, elec-

Atwater Hotel, Avalon.

trically-lit cottages with rugs, double beds, dressers, and chairs. Mr. Wrigley insisted that the linen in the bungalettes be changed every day, thereby creating a need for a laundry, one of the island's first businesses. There was even a ball park, built as a training ground for his beloved Cubs.

Early in 1920 Mr. Wrigley decided that a new hotel was needed to take care of guests who could afford more luxurious accommodations. David Renton was given a challenge: build a new hotel before the summer season opened in June. Accomplishing this on the mainland would have been difficult enough, but on an island it seemed unthinkable, to all but Messrs. Wrigley and Renton, that is. The new Hotel Atwater, named for Philip Wrigley's wife Helen Atwater, was completed on time.

Another lure for tourists was the Bird Park, that housed one of the greatest collections of rare and exotic birds in the world. The idea of building the park was not Mr. Wrigley's (a mainland bird enthusiast had proposed the idea to him), but he recognized the commercial potential of such a venture and paid for the construction of cages and the first specimens. Although it never brought in any direct revenue, the Bird Park was designed to attract families and was touted in the island's advertising.

Mr. Wrigley spent much of his personal fortune to upgrade Catalina for tourists, but he was also concerned with the welfare of the island's permanent residents. A variety of new businesses were created not only to assist with the island's development, but

Old Catalina Bird Park.

to provide employment. Construction of the hotel and the bungalettes resulted in the establishment of several island industries. Obtaining furniture for the guest quarters proved irritatingly difficult, but David Renton was able to solve the problem. In 1920 he closed his mainland construction business and moved all his equipment and tools to Avalon. Near the present-day location of the school he set up a furniture shop, later moved to Pebbly Beach.

The Pebbly Beach rock quarry that had been used since early 1900 provided crushed rock and gravel for road construction; tons of material was also barged to the mainland to be used in the Long Beach breakwater. This also meant additional revenue and jobs for island dwellers. There was a forge at Pebbly

Beach run by a stocky Scot named Llewellen Mc-Intire which serviced the quarry, the Renton mine and heavy equipment, as well as the local horses. In 1926 a water pipeline was completed that linked the reservoir to the town of Avalon. The local newspaper *The Catalina Islander* headlined the advent of fresh water for residents and tourists.

By the early 1920s there was one more new and exciting business for Messrs. Wrigley and Renton. Its origin is one of Catalina's most enduring legends, told here by Malcolm Renton.

☐ Mr. William Wrigley was out with my father, David Renton. They were up in the golf course area driving around in the wet weather and got stuck in the clay — the adobe. Somehow, my father got his hands in the clay and

William Wrigley, Jr.'s Arabian horse ranch, Catalina.

Tile floor in Philip K. Wrigley residence, Avalon.

Hillside erosion on the site of the first clay pit.

Early plant operation at Pebbly Beach, 1920s.

said "Maybe this would be good enough to make bricks." Mr. Wrigley told my dad, "Check it out. Go ahead and see what you can do." And that was the start of Catalina tile. [3]

The clay from the golf course area proved to have the plasticity, shrinkage, tensile strength and fusibility to be useful. Another source of Catalina commerce was born, and a plant for making brick and tile was added to the growing "industrial complex" at Pebbly Beach.

A ceramics plant could accommodate both skilled and unskilled labor, a place where a variety of people would be able to find jobs. Mr. Wrigley also knew that using native materials in the construction of new buildings would save money and add to the many unique qualities Catalina already possessed and wasted no time in developing the new facility. Catalina clay came primarily from four places on the island. One can still see marks in the land between the golf course and the Avalon school where the first clay was dug out. Echo Lake at the summit of Black Jack Mountain above Avalon, Renton Pass, Little Harbor and the western end of Catalina held other large concentrations of clay. They were found to be of the "red-burning" variety, well suited for making bricks, the first products of the new enterprise.

Although neither man had experience with brick-making, both Wrigley and Renton realized the importance of using local talent whenever possible and bringing in experienced people from the mainland when necessary. The town of Avalon provided a great variety of people and skills to draw upon.

Johnnie Windle is an Avalonite who started to work for Mr. Wrigley as a messenger boy in 1919. He was made Superintendent of Transportation in 1923 and given responsibility for all material import and export. As he explained, "All hauling, no matter

24

Red clay pavers with Catalina tiles.

whether by boat, by barge or by land was done by men I supervised. Even the actual digging of the clay and delivering it to the mill . . . at Pebbly Beach."[4]

The newly-created plant may have begun producing brick as early as 1923. The process of making raw clay into finished bricks began as soon as Johnnie Windle's crew had taken a load of clay to the plant at Pebbly Beach.

The raw material was pulverized in a ball mill, then mixed with water to the proper consistency and pressed by hand into brick molds and set aside to dry. The men who filled the molds went home at night with very sore hands. The dried bricks were fired in field kilns, small oil furnaces built outside adjacent to the plant. Firing took many hours and the result was brick of a magnificent red color.

The plant made three types of face brick. Accord-

Early patio tile design.

Mold for patio floor tile.

ing to an old company catalogue, they were called "Avalon Tapestry," "Catalina Bark," and "Descanso Tapestry." Some of the early brick can be seen in Avalon to this day: for instance, the teeth of the snake in the Serpent Wall on Crescent Avenue are made of "Avalon Tapestry" brick.

Next in the product line were hollow tiles used in construction and patio tiles or pavers. The latter were especially popular. In his interview, Johnnie described "a whole room with nothing but molds of different designs for patio floor tile. I used to watch them do all that because anything we hauled in we also hauled out."

Many Catalina homes have patios made of these early, still beautiful, floor tiles. The best examples of the patio floor tiles can be seen at the Casino and also in the patio of the Country Club.

The product line also included clay roofing or "Mission" tiles. The Mission Revival style spawned a thriving business all over California for the curved red roof tiles, and the clay works readily accommodated mainland customers. Mission tiles also graced Mr. William Wrigley's home in Phoenix that overlooked his famous Arizona Biltmore Hotel.

Graham Brothers in Long Beach was the company's outlet for mainland sales as business began to expand beyond Catalina. As Malcolm Renton remembered,

☐ "We got going so well that we started to expand and sell to mainland sources. We had a yard at Graham Brothers, which was primarily a rock plant operation in Long Beach. From there my dad had salesmen that would go out and try to sell our products. My dad was a good friend of Dr. Edmond, President of Pomona College. At that time Clark Hall, a new dormitory, was being built and my dad convinced his friend to use Catalina tile for all of the porches, hallways, and the roof.

"After we graduated from the rough, early type of tile [in the late 1920s], we got into the regular glazed tile. The ramps at the old Long Beach Auditorium were covered with Catalina tile. And there was glazed tile of all different colors, blues, red and so forth on the walls.[5]

In the early 1930s, a line of dinnerware and decorative pottery was being produced. William Wrigley, Jr. was surprised and pleased to find that the pottery was profitable. Before long Catalina pottery and the popular dinnerware were out-selling the tile. However, Mr. Wrigley was in the midst of a number of construction projects on Catalina and in Arizona, and the brick, Mission, and glazed tile were to become an integral part of these projects.

William Wrigley (left) with David Renton, the Catalina Country Club, c. 1928.

CATALINA POTTERY HEYDAY

Management of the pottery was in the capable hands of Philip K. Wrigley and General Manager David Renton. Catalina Island had benefited materially and economically from the bricks, pavers and roof tiles produced by the plant, and it is probable that the men of the Santa Catalina

29

Catalina clay products at Casa Descanso, Catalina.

Chimes Tower, Avalon.

Catalina tile table and Indian design vase.

Island Company saw many advantages to producing decorative tile. Also, Philip K. Wrigley had a grand plan for the island's architecture and ambience, in which tile would play an integral part.

He told his biographer, "The historic background of Catalina Island . . . its natural beauty and romance lend themselves admirably to the preservation of the atmosphere of old California. Being an island, we can control a definite plan over a period of years, unhampered by outside commercialism . . . Gradually we may be able to make all of Catalina Island a monument to the early beginnings of California." [6]

Catalina clays in various mixtures were well suited to the many kinds of ceramic products that came from the plant. Experiment revealed the best combinations for decorative tile: the clay had to be plastic enough to be malleable and the shrinkage accurately gauged. By this time, the employees at the plant had developed an eye and a feel for the clays, and the correct clay "recipe" was soon put into production.

The rock quarry near the tile plant produced great quantities of dust that were a health hazard. Philip Wrigley and David Renton devised a unique way to protect the plant workers and at the same time found a use for the airborne dust. It was collected on screens, gathered in bags and later added to the clay being prepared for tile production. This same system was used in the early 1930s when the plant began making hand-thrown pottery, christened "Pottery from the Air" by Los Angeles newspaper reporters.

The tile plant's largest job was an important one for Catalina: the magnificent new Casino. Mr. Wrigley had originally built a dance pavilion in 1920 for the enjoyment of the island's residents and guests, but he knew that he could oblige even greater numbers of tourists by building a larger facility. The old structure was dismantled in February 1928, and its steel frame became the home for the exotic birds at the Catalina Bird Park.

The new Casino was designed to outshine what had stood there before, and the tile plant played an important role in creating the aura of elegance that became the building's trademark. Patio and roofing tiles (105,000 of the latter) were used on the exterior, and decorative glazed tile inside.

The seascape murals in the Casino's portico were originally designed to be made of glazed Catalina tile. John Gabriel Beckman, who had recently completed the interior design for Grauman's Chinese Theatre in Hollywood, was asked by the Santa Catalina Island Company to decorate the grand Casino. However, because of time constraints on the project, it was eventually decided that the murals would be painted directly on a prepared surface. In 1986, nearly 50 years later, the decision was made to recreate the murals in their originally intended tiled format. Mainland tilemaker Richard Keit, working with Beckman as a consultant, redesigned the center mural from an old black and white photograph and then produced the design on 8 x 8-inch tiles specially made for the project by Dal-Tile Corporation.

The Casino with Catalina roofing tiles.

Stenton Wilcox installing tiles in Casino's new murals.

The famed Casino Ballroom featured a magnificent soda fountain decorated with Catalina tiles in shades of turquoise, silver and apricot. The building's foyer was made with the plant's patio tiles.

Other locations in Avalon were enhanced by the use of Catalina tile. The Security Pacific Bank building at Crescent Avenue and Claressa, the Serpent Wall which snakes along the front street, the telephone company building, the Chime Tower, numerous storefronts and the airport all still display the local tile placed there in the 1930s. The fountain at the foot of the original steamer pier was made with Catalina tile, providing disembarking passengers with a lovely tiled view as they first set foot on the island. (The tiles on the outside of the fountain are new.)

Tile installations on Crescent Avenue shops facing Avalon Bay.

The walls of the men's room at the Country Club are decorated with varicolored and variously designed tiles, a reflection of the whimsy of the tile setter who was limited by the odd lots of tiles at hand. One of the most notable installations of decorative glazed tiles can still be seen at the Wrigley Memorial overlooking the canyon outside of Avalon.

Many private homes, including Philip K. Wrigley's magnificent Mediterranean-style home overlooking Avalon Bay, contain examples of the tile plant's products. The exterior of the house is adorned with both roofing and patio tiles; the walkways, fountains and planters show evidence of the plant's colorful output. Decorative materials from other local industries were also used, such as wrought-iron

Terrace at the Philip K. Wrigley residence, Avalon.

Philip K. Wrigley residence, Avalon.

grilles and ornaments made at Catalina's forge or machine shops.

Everyday objects made with tile are today regarded as among the most valuable items produced by the plant, and the most coveted are the Catalina tables. Some table bases were made of wood from the furniture factory under the direction of James Ramsey. A fine furniture maker, Ramsey also built the beautiful staircase in Mrs. Wrigley's home on Mt. Ada. The first wrought iron table bases with feet shaped like inverted spoons were made at the machine shop. The shop was at the end of Pebbly Beach, where the Buffalo Nickel Cafe stands today. According to Earl Limbeck, who worked at the shop:

☐ The very first tables that we made were with ¼″ wrought iron bars that we bent, and those tables were riveted. We only used ¼″, and ⅝″ iron depending on the size of

Square Catalina tile table with Catalina candy dish.

Octagon tile table design.

the table. For the larger tables, the umbrella tables, ¾″ was used. Later we welded them. We only made about three styles and would vary the height and make minor changes in the design.[7]

Other tables bases were of cast iron, a mainland product. The plant's sales manager Frank Trimble had connections with a Los Angeles foundry and arranged to have these cast bases shipped to Catalina Island. The tile-covered tops were attached in the machine shop where the pieces were either riveted or welded together. Limbeck said, "We didn't have any drawings. Frank would just say, "Well, do it like this," or he would draw a few lines on a paper. There were never any dimensions. You made everything out of your head. From the start to the end there weren't more than a dozen leg styles."

Earl remembers David Renton well, recalling, among other things, that he always wore a hat and always walked with his hands in his pockets, except when driving his green LaSalle roadster. In the early 1930s Earl was transferred from the machine shop to the power plant, located in Falls Canyon.

One day, after the delivery of a new generator, David Renton came by to see how things were going. Just before he arrived the oil lines in the new appliance suddenly ruptured, sending bolts flying through the air and spewing oil all over the floor. Mr. Renton walked into the building, his hands in his pockets; and before anyone could warn him, he stepped down into the room where the generator was located, slipped in the oil and fell. Much to Earl's surprise, he quickly got up, turned around and walked out without uttering a word.

The tiled tops of the iron tables were either silk screened or hand painted. The outline of the design was often applied by a traditional method known as "pouncing." A pattern was created by punching tiny holes onto a parchment-like material placed on damp tile. A cloth was dipped into a dry mineral oxide which was then dabbed on the holes. The oxide sifted through the holes onto the clay, and the glazer then filled in between the lines according to a predetermined color scheme. As *The Catalina Islander* described:

☐ Each piece is hand-decorated by pretty Catalina girls, trained in the art of applying the varied colored glazes. Instead of using a brush, the 'painting' is done with a small syringe, which is dipped in a series of receptacles, each

Tile table with rare handpainted desert scene displayed at the golf course, Catalina, c. 1930.

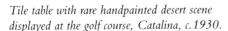

containing a different mineral oxide. The pattern is marked out on the tile and great care must be taken that each glaze stays within the 'dead line' and does not flow over, or the whole design is spoiled. It is most interesting to watch these clever girls as with deft fingers they apply the multi-colored glazes, for strangely the colors are quite different from what they turn out to be after they are burned in the kiln — a pink may be obsidian black and a delicate blue will come out a yellow.[8]

The tile was then dried and fired for a second time to fuse the glaze to the surface.

Many of the designs used on the tables as well as on other tile products were inspired by the natural beauty of the island. Birds, seascapes, native plants, flying fish, swordfish, and other sea creatures all came to life on Catalina tiled tables. There were as many table tops as there were tile designs: decorative bird tables, one of the most popular items; backgammon tables, reportedly made at the request of Mrs. William Wrigley; revolving bookcases with tiled tops, made either with plain or decorated tile; as well as occasional, lamp, and coffee tables.

Alma Overholt, Mr. Wrigley's Catalina Island publicist, wrote many articles about the tile and pottery works for the local newspaper *The Catalina Islander*. Her flowery descriptions may occasionally verge on hyperbole, but they give a delightful glimpse into the mystique of the island.

☐ To go with the coffee table is the tile-top bridge table — one of the most strikingly beautiful of these tables comes in toyon red and obsidian black checker-board motif with the

Backgammon tabletop of Catalina tiles.

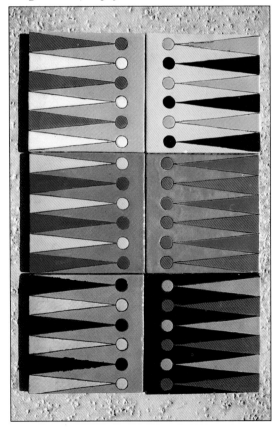

four card motifs, one in each corner done in gold-leaf—burned under the glaze. And quite the newest and most smart are the tile-top backgammon tables—the game itself burned into the tile as the design and the "checkers" to be played with, also of little round tiles.[9]

Birds were a favorite motif for tables and tile murals. Many of them were the creation of Roger "Bud" Upton, a Catalina artist for over 60 years. He was born in Massachusetts in 1900 and came to Catalina for the first time in 1902; his family spent summers on the island and winters in Pasadena. By the 1920s he dominated the art scene on Catalina, and in 1932 Bud and his wife Betty became permanent residents of Avalon, where he set up his own business. He found a place for himself at the tile plant, where he designed numerous pottery pieces and tiles. As birds were one of his specialties, he designed tiles for the tables and plaques. He recalled,

☐ how important it was to differentiate between the various liquid glazes when working with the tile. There are different kinds of glazes, but all look alike when liquid. The only way to tell the difference is to read the labels on the containers. For instance, blue might not look blue until after it's fired.[10]

Bud was renowned locally for his paintings as well as his tile designs. The Wrigley family commissioned many of his works to hang in the various offices throughout the country.

Another employee of the Wrigley Company was Otis Shepard, who worked mainly out of Chicago

Tile mural, Two Toucans.

Green Macaw, single bird design.

Window sill, telephone company building, Catalina.

Head of serpent wall on Crescent Avenue, Avalon.

and New York and was the firm's chief artist. He was sent to Catalina to lend his expert eye and experience to the development of Avalon. It was his idea to make the wall on Crescent Avenue into a serpentine shape, and he was responsible for the design of the street itself. Shepard also conceived of the plan to use Catalina tile seconds to decorate the sea wall and the planter boxes there. In addition, he designed the masthead for *The Catalina Islander.*

Manufacturing ceramic tile called for additional expertise. Building the facilities for production, decorating and glazing no doubt presented a challenge to those in charge. Throughout the years after the tile plant was established, the Santa Catalina Island Company consulted and hired trained ceramists. Among those hired in 1932 was John Wilde, the son of Fred H. Wilde, a renowned ceramist from England who

Old Bird Park fountain relocated to Avalon Plaza.

had a long and fruitful career with a number of American tile companies. Fred Wilde had ended his career at the Pomona Tile Manufacturing Company near Los Angeles, where his son John was also employed.

Legend has it that John Wilde was a "color man," having inherited from his father both the ability and the recipes for creating distinctive glazes. He is remembered for being an expert in blues, greens and reds, significant colors for Catalina tiles. John was "loaned" by the proprietors at Pomona. It's possible that, due to the Depression, the Pomona company might have had trouble paying him, yet the company may not have liked the idea of losing a valuable employee. By "loaning" him, the company could be reasonably assured that he would return during better economic times.

Wilde and his wife moved to Catalina, and John began his duties as plant supervisor in charge of production. In the summer of 1932 he offered a job to John Calvin Tyler, the son of family friends. Tyler came to the island for an interview and was put through the most rigorous questioning process he had ever experienced. Apparently the presence of young girls in the tile plant made the Santa Catalina Island Company extremely cautious about the morals of the young men hired. Tyler was approved and moved in with the Wildes, who, having no children of their own, treated him like family.

Tyler was responsible for stenciling designs on 10″ x 10″ pavers and for some glazing. It was a tedious job, but he knew it was only for the summer, and he had the evenings at the Casino to look forward to. John remembers with happiness dancing in the grand ballroom. He was grateful for his summer on Catalina, for it allowed him to save enough money to go to college.

John Wilde stayed on Catalina until 1936. He became factory superintendent and eventually went to work for Gladding, McBean and Company which shortly was to play an important role in the history of the Catalina clay works.

Another person whose youth was closely affiliated with the tile company was Gloria Lopez. Born and raised on Catalina, after graduating from Avalon High School she began work as a finisher at the factory, where she earned $16 a week. Her job was to prepare the tiles for the kiln; she also did some glaze

Square and octagon patio tiles.

work. She remembers that an assembly line was used when a large order of tile was being produced. First, one or two colors were applied to the tiles that were then set aside to dry. Other colors were added in the same manner. The glazers had to be careful that the colors wouldn't run together. She also remembers that the tiles were very fragile before firing and broke easily. Once fired, defective tiles were discarded or sold as seconds.

Wrigley Memorial with view toward the sea.

The work that Gloria performed was difficult and exacting; but she was enthusiastic, and the presence of other young women made the day go quickly. Each morning, a group of girls would meet at the end of Crescent Avenue and walk to the plant together. In the winter, when the seas were rough, waves occasionally washed over the road or would hit the rocks at the edge and spray the road with salt water. The girls would run frantically to avoid getting wet, laughing gaily when someone got caught by the spray. In describing her years at the tile plant Gloria said, "It was a great life. I had a wonderful time."

Bernice Limbeck, Earl's sister, joined her family in Avalon after graduating from high school in 1932. At Earl's suggestion she applied for employment at the pottery works and was soon decorating tiles.

☐ I decorated many tiles that were used in the Wrigley Memorial. We made thousands of them. I have looked back on it many times and feel that the small group that I worked with must have been hired specifically for that project. We worked hard, but we all cooperated and there was always time for fun. There wasn't the stress and pressure that people complain of today. When time permitted we all made special items for ourselves. I remember my husband, Don Ruth. He wasn't my husband then; we didn't get married until after I had left the tile plant. Don was the mold maker. He made special little molds for buttons just for me. I still have them.[12]

A very attractive young woman, Bernice posed for many of the publicity pictures taken at that time. Photographs of her showing the steps in decorating tile were used in the Catalina pottery display at the Chicago World's Fair in 1933. Bernice was one of the group that used to meet at the end of Crescent Avenue and walk to Pebbly Beach, but she readily admitted, "I got a ride whenever I could."

By the early 1930s the tile factory was an impres-

Visitors watch Bernice Limbeck apply color glazes to bisque tiles.

Interior, Wrigley Memorial, Catalina.

sive operation including artists' studios, research laboratories, molding rooms, kilns, assembling rooms and open air dryers. Glazing rooms and laboratories, a cellar, a second story molding room and a substantial storage yard completed the plant at the height of operations.

The fame of Catalina ceramics was spreading due in part to the use of the tile at various locations owned by the Wrigleys. The swimming pool at the Arizona Biltmore in Phoenix featured a spectacular installation of Catalina tiles. The hotel had been opened in 1929 just before the October stock market crash, and, when the original builders lost the hotel it was acquired by William Wrigley. In the early 1930s the magnificent pool was added to the hotel complex. Its tiled sides, bottom and curb were made exclusively of Catalina tile: 4″ x 4″ and 6″ x 6″ tiles of cobalt blue, yellow and green. Below the waterline was a row of 6″ x 6″ tiles decorated with a tulip-like design, also in the same colors but outlined in black. The scum gutter, coping and tile curb repeated the tulip decoration along with a filler of solid colors. In 1971, the tiles at and above the waterline were replaced with precise reproductions.

The diving board housing at the east end of the pool was decorated with bird murals set in the walls, and the nearby bathhouse was tiled throughout. The Wrigleys also built a winter home overlooking the hotel. Catalina tile was used extensively on the floors, on the fireplace facades, and in the many bathrooms, each with its own color scheme.

Catalina tile installations, Arizona Biltmore pool.

*Chicago Cub players Mack
Kuykendall and Chuck Klein
with "Cat-O-Lina" pottery
planters, cactus salt and pepper
shakers, and bears.*

*Publicity shot of Cubs Leroy
Herrman, Bill Lee, and Gordon
Phelps pushing rail cart of plates
to the kilns, c.1934.*

*Pottery Shop on Crescent Avenue
in the 1930s.*

Long Beach, California, has a small residential section known as the "Wrigley District." Mr. Wrigley had established a building company called Fleming and Weber soon after his purchase of Catalina Island, and this company purchased ten acres in Long Beach. Although the area was mostly swamp, the city's new run-off drains eventually made it usable. The land was subdivided into lots and sold, and even though Mr. Wrigley never took an active part in the business, his name remained when the houses were built. Most of the homes on the 2000 and 2100 blocks of Eucalyptus Street were built by Wrigley company builders who used Catalina products.

The Santa Catalina Island Company promoted the use of its ceramic products. The Casino Way Pottery Shop in Avalon was one of a number of retail stores on the island. There was an elaborate display area at the Casino where tile and pottery were sold. The Catalina Ceramics Shop on popular Olvera Street in Los Angeles was the primary mainland outlet, and there was also a shop at the Arizona Biltmore. The tiles and pottery were sold in department stores from coast to coast.

Advertising for the pottery products was placed in newspapers and magazines written in the flowery style of the era.

CATALINA POTTERY AND TILE

Offers Something New In Ceramics, Of Interest To All Concerned In Buildings And Furnishing Architects and builders will find Catalina tile most beautiful and useful in lending itself admirably to California Architecture. Made on Catalina Island of Catalina materials it is "a little bit of the Magic Isle"— a charming souvenir of California's favorite seaside outing place.[13]

By the early 1930s the plant was called "Catalina Clay Products" and was issuing detailed price lists. The 1931 issue was typed, with handwritten corrections. It listed patio tile, half and diagonal tiles, brick, hollow, Mission roof and drain tile, glazed trimmers, hand made faience and glazed grilles and vents. The art pottery and dinnerware had a separate catalog and price list.

In 1934, the price list was typeset and printed, showing the addresses of the sales office and display rooms in Los Angeles at 323 Pacific Electric Building and 618 No. Main Street, respectively. It listed prices for Plain and Decorative Panels, Embossed and Decorative Tea Tiles, as well as the standard hollow, drain and roof items. The list of Bird Panels is a tantalizing peek at the variety of designs available: Modern Bird, Toucan, Green Macaw (Single Bird), Red Macaw

Catalina tile installation on Avalon storefront.

(Double Bird), Crested Crane, Parakeet and Oval Bird (Black and Gold). Non-bird motifs are also given in the same section: Desert Scene, Madonna, Madonna and Child (Hand Painted), Swordfish and Mermaid (Octagon). Interestingly, the name of the business venture was given as the Clay Products Division of the Santa Catalina Island Company, not Catalina Clay Products as in the 1931 price sheets. The back page of the visually sophisticated 1934 catalog has charming Catalina Island logos with the motto, "In All The World No Trip Like This."

Green Macaw bird mural

The C.R. Kayser Company represented the tile to dealers and at trade shows and expositions. In 1932 Catalina tables were, in Alma Overholt's words, "the sensation" of the Furniture Show in Los Angeles. In 1933 the plant held an exhibit at the Chicago World's Fair that included not only the ceramic products but a large relief map of Catalina Island as well. The last known exhibit of pottery products was at the Panama Pacific Exposition in San Diego in 1935, although the tile wasn't represented. Sadly, even though the popularity of Catalina's unique and beautiful ware was at its height, the plant itself would soon be only a memory.

Catalina pottery with rare handpainted bird plate with black glaze.

Catalina tile and pottery in various functional forms.

LAST DAYS OF THE POTTERY

The early 1930s brought many changes to the island and the tile plant. On January 26, 1932 William Wrigley, Jr. died peacefully at his home in Phoenix at the age of seventy. Though his death had no material effect on the life of the island — Philip K. Wrigley was president of the Santa Catalina

Red Macaw, double bird panel.

Island Company—his passing deeply affected those residents who remembered him and how he brought about Catalina's renaissance.

By 1932 the people in charge of production at the ceramics plant realized that local clays did not have the strength needed to create truly sturdy tile and art pottery. Despite its beauty, the clayware chipped and broke easily. In an attempt to strengthen its products the company experimented with adding talc that was found in plentiful supply at Renton Pass. Talc had become increasingly popular among ceramists during the 1920s, but the results at Catalina did not meet the company's expectations. A white clay was subsequently imported from Lincoln, California, about 30 miles northeast of Sacramento. The addition of this clay adequately solved the chipping problem but created a new one. The cost of importing the clay to the island was prohibitive, and even with the newer, stronger product, there continued to be a high incidence of breakage.

As the years passed, there was a gradual waning of interest in Catalina's clay products. With the rising tide of the Great Depression, it became clear that the plant could no longer turn a profit. In addition, with the death of William Wrigley, Jr. and completion of the Arizona Biltmore and the Wrigley home in Phoenix, the company lost its biggest tile customer. Once the tiles for the Memorial were completed in 1934, orders for tile diminished and the demise of the plant became apparent. In my interview with Malcolm Renton, he reminisced that "some island residents

Tile bathroom, Wrigley Residence, Phoenix.

William Wrigley, Jr. memorial, Catalina Island.

Catalina cribbage board.

Tile roof of El Encanto.

Tile detail in Wrigley residence, Phoenix.

were able to take advantage of the opportunity to pick up Catalina tile of their own. Toward the end there were a couple of buildings at Pebbly Beach that had boxes of remnants, the old stuff, and these tiles gradually were spread all over town. People would help themselves to it. If you see it on flower boxes or on stairs in some of the side streets it would be some of that original Catalina tile." [14]

The Santa Catalina Island Company began negotiating with Gladding, McBean and Company in 1936 to take over the ceramics plant. Approaching this established clay business as a purchaser was a logical and practical move.

Gladding, McBean was founded in 1875 in Lincoln, California, where the white clay that had strengthened Catalina clay products originated. In 1884 the firm began to produce architectural terra cotta, a popular material among builders and architects of the time. Beginning with hollow tile, the company moved on to face brick, roof tile, other forms of brick and, in 1923, glazed ceramic tile. By the late 1920s the firm was one of the largest ceramic manufacturing companies in the United States.

The Santa Catalina Island Company initially suggested that Gladding, McBean lease the production facilities at Pebbly Beach and continue to produce the Catalina pottery on the island. This proposal didn't interest the mainland firm; the high cost of importing clay had caused the problem in the first place. However, in March of 1937, an agreement was reached: Gladding, McBean purchased the molds and the

Catalina pottery with handpainted buffalo plate.

Collectable Catalina dinnerware.

rights to the Catalina name for $50,000 and transferred all production to the mainland. The agreement was to last a minimum of ten years. However, the production of decorative glazed tile ended when the island plant closed.

For two years Gladding, McBean made the commercially successful Catalina dinnerware at its Glendale facility. By World War II, items identified as Catalina Pottery were being phased out and integrated into Gladding, McBean's popular "Franciscan" line. After the war, relations between the two firms changed again as the ten-year agreement period came to an end.

□ Since the beginning of the war it has not been possible for Gladding, McBean and Company to manufacture art pottery of any description and we were forced to discon-

Gladding, McBean shallow flower bowl with Richard Keit reproduction tiles.

tinue the use of the trade name "Catalina." We are not in a position at present to manufacture art pottery and with the large number of potteries that have started in Southern California in the last few years, the art pottery business is not attractive for a firm such as ours. Therefore, we will not have need to renew our agreement with you and hereby resign all rights to the trade name "Catalina" as applied to pottery products.[15]

In 1947 Gladding, McBean returned the use of the trademark to the Santa Catalina Island Company. An attempt to revive the production of brick on the island in 1963 was not successful.

As time passed, the tile installations on Catalina became an unnoticed part of the landscape; everyone knew the tiles were there, but few people recalled the unique circumstances under which they had been made. Boxes of tiles carried away by island residents

Bird tile flower boxes, old Banning residence.

for future use were placed in attics or store rooms or given away as gifts. No one imagined that the glazed or decorated objects of clay would ever have more than nostalgic value. However, within the last few years, interest in the American art pottery movement and the decorative tiles of the 1920s and 1930s—including Catalina—has been revived among collectors and enthusiastic amateurs.

Unfortunately, the zeal to collect Catalina tiles has resulted in numerous incidents of vandalism on the island. The remains of the Bird Park — closed in the early 1970s—show the unmistakable signs of profiteers. Pieces of broken tiles lie in various places on the grounds. Whole tiles have been carted away after being chipped roughly away from their settings. Other locations on Catalina Island have suffered similar fates, even though, by themselves, the stolen tiles have little or no monetary value away from their original placement. Pollution and the normal effects of weather have also had a deleterious effect on outdoor installations.

☐ Some Catalina tile projects have had more pleasant fates. The Arizona Biltmore remained in the Wrigley family after its acquisition in 1929. The family had always been careful to see that the unique architectural elements of the hotel were preserved, and in 1971 attention was turned to the swimming pool. The manager wanted to renovate it and replace all the tile above the water line, at the same time retaining the design and colors of the original Catalina tile. Facings of America, a tile distributor in Phoenix, agreed to do the job to the management's exacting specifications. In cooperation with Kraftile Co. of Fremont, California, the

Tile installation, Miller Art Tile

Modern Bird, also known as "Fantasy Bird."

Catalina designs and colors were recreated so closely that, once installed, the reproductions are indistinguishable from the originals.[16]

Concurrent with the rise in interest and prices is a preservation effort spearheaded by enlightened collectors and organizations such as the Tile Heritage Foundation. Through lectures, bulletins, and magazine and newspaper articles, individuals and groups are beginning to make the public aware of the importance of our ceramic heritage.

Catalina tables, murals and single decorative tiles rank high in the catalogue of American art tile. The unique circumstance of their creation, the beauty of the surroundings in which they were made and installed and the danger they now face place Catalina tiles on the list of our most precious ceramic legacies. Education can make the uninitiated aware of the fragile nature of ceramic surfaces. When preservation efforts are undertaken before damage occurs or when funds are made available for restoration as needed, America's ceramic heritage can be protected and preserved.

Today, many colorful installations of Catalina tile remain on the island. Conceived by a benevolent millionaire and brought to life by skilled hands, Catalina tile represents a unique part of the history of decorative arts in America for present and future generations to enjoy.

CATALINA TILES FOR THE COLLECTOR

Collecting is one of the most popular hobbies in America today. Whether indoors in antique stores and collectives or outdoors at garage sales and flea markets, collecting can be a mad, expensive scramble or a well thought out economical pursuit. Most of all, it is something anyone can do; the collector is in

67

Catalina tile table with island pottery.

complete charge and makes all the rules. Along with this freedom comes the responsibility for discipline and education.

Identifying Catalina tile is not an easy task. The number of former plant workers knowledgeable about the tile diminishes each year, and the identifying marks cannot be examined once tiles have been installed. Enthusiasts must therefore rely on the work of experts or do considerable research on their own to identify a tile and discern the date of its manufacture. A trip to Catalina Island is a necessity for a serious collector. In fact, many people have started their collections after visiting the island and seeing the many beautiful examples of the tile and pottery.

Today, Mr. Malcolm Renton is one of the most reliable sources of information about the tile on Catalina. "All the buildings built by the company used tile made on the island. We would not have allowed any other tile on the island, and we were in a position to control that." The only way to make a reasonably accurate accounting of Catalina tile designs would be to trace all the varying tiles on the known company buildings. Even that would not necessarily be a complete list, for it is possible that other tile patterns were made. In addition, the collector must be aware that tile patterns and designs were not all exclusive to Catalina. Many tile makers of that era were using very similar, if not identical, patterns. Hence, one should also try to identify glazes, styles of designs and types of manufacture.

One clue to the age of a piece of Catalina tile or

Cupola from old Hamilton Beach airport, restored with RTK Studio tiles.

pottery is the color of the clay body. The first products of the plant were made exclusively of local clays that were deep red or brown. These can be dated from 1927–1932. Once the production of the art pottery got underway, many tiles contained a white mainland clay that was added to the local mixture; the result was a lighter clay color. These date from 1932–1937, though darker clay was used concurrently with the white until around 1935. The art pottery can be dated similarly; once the dinnerware was put in production, all of the pottery was produced with a white clay body.

Each tile should have a stamped "Catalina" on the back, but Mr. Renton admits that workers were sometimes lax and had to be reminded to stamp the tiles. Some bricks were stamped with a small "Catalina," as well. However, with bricks set in place and grouted, these helpful marks are no longer visible.

Glaze colors are another clue to the identification and dating of Catalina tile. In the early years, there were only a few basic colors: Catalina Blue, Descanso Green, Black, White, Mandarin Yellow, Monterey Brown and the most striking of all, Toyon Red. Light Green, Light Blue, Old Rose and Orchid were added a few years later. A pottery price list dated November 1, 1936 — the last one printed by the plant — listed Matte Blue, Matte Green, Toyon Red (always a favorite), Mandarin Yellow, Pearly White, Turquoise, Powder Blue, Colonial Yellow and Coral Island.

There has been much speculation among collectors about the formulas for the beautiful Catalina

Drinking fountain at the Catalina Country Club.

Blue glaze Catalina pottery.

glazes; for glaze recipes were well guarded secrets. Although Malcolm Renton believes that there was a formula book at one time, it has not yet been found. The "Toyon Red" glaze, White and Flesh or Beige, however, are known to contain uranium oxide. From *Ceramic Glazes* written in 1948:

URANIUM OXIDE. Colors ranging from a light yellow to a deep orange may be had with uranium oxide according to the amount used and the bases present. About 10% of sodium uranate is needed for the deepest color. The alkaline earths do not affect the color; the alkalies, including lithia, lighten the color. Ivory colored shades may be produced by the addition of 6% tin oxide and 1 to 2% of sodium uranate to a lead glaze containing zinc oxide..Uranium oxide is a reliable reagent for producing reds...

Uranium oxide was not a local product, so it must have been brought onto the island. It was commonly used by ceramists of that day, and evidence of its use can be found in Bauer, Franciscan, Rancho and other popular pottery manufactured until the end of World War II when other glaze ingredients were substituted.

Much of the tile used for table tops was produced for round tops: six pentagon-shaped tiles with a hexagon at the center made up a complete set. Another popular design was a circle intersected with two parallel lines at right angles to each other. This created a square tile in the center with four pie-shaped tiles in the corners and four tiles with three straight sides and one rounded. These shapes can be seen decorating the outside walls of many homes on Catalina as well as installed in tables. Other round

Poinsettia table being restored.

Casa Descanso patio with inlaid tiles.

designs were made by putting four tiles together which had been cut in the shape of a quarter-circle. Combinations of four, six or fifteen (as in the case of the airplane designs) were also used.

Custom designed tables were made in addition to the regular line. There were at least two desert scenes: one showed a mounted Indian on a cliff overlooking the desert with a covered wagon in the distance, and the other, a scene of saguaro cactus. Undersea garden

Unset table tiles.

scenes were very popular, as well as a Poinsettia, a swordfish, various birds and airplanes. Mr. Wrigley's Casino was also featured in both a multi-tiled mural and as a single enlarged tile. These are extremely rare.

Collectors must keep in mind the great variety of styles and sizes of Catalina tables; these include coffee tables, card tables, and even umbrella styles for patios. All came in differing sizes; plain and decorative tiles were used. Sets of tiles were also sold for the convenience of travelers who wanted to take them home for their own use.

As there is no known illustrated pattern catalog for the furniture, it is difficult to know with certainty that a particular table was made on Catalina. Islanders, as well as the local museum, have tables that are considered authentic. However, many tiles were sold to mainlanders who carried them away; some

Tile installation, Wrigley residence, Phoenix.

Small star tile table.

may have been set into tables made elsewhere. One reliable method is to examine the way the base and the table top have been attached. With some Catalina wooden tables, the tops were completed and the tile set before the legs were attached. The tile tops were attached by using metal "figure eights": one of the circular pieces was imbedded in the leg and apron of the table base and the other was attached with a screw to the underside of the table top.

The tiles and pottery manufactured at the plant on Catalina have been distributed over the years to all parts of the country both by visiting tourists returning home and by the vigorous sales force of the Wrigley organization. If not broken or thrown away during the intervening years, these various clay products can still be found and the hunt for these "survivors" can be a rewarding and satisfying pursuit.

Tile maker Richard Keit with completed mural, one of three planned for the Casino.

CATALINA TILES
DESIGN GUIDE

Tile wall in the Country Club mens room.

This guide was created to help collectors locate and identify authentic Catalina tiles. Tracings were made from tile installations on Santa Catalina Island Company buildings on the island and from private collections. Not all designs produced by the pottery are represented, but the guide includes most patterns made up to 1934.

PARAKEETS (DOUBLE BIRD)
     FROM 1934 CATALOG
    HAND DECORATED

GREEN MACAW
(SINGLE BIRD) TWO TOUCANS

MARLIN —
ONE TILE SMALLER
THAN 6 INCHES

MODERN BIRD
OR "FANTASY BIRD"

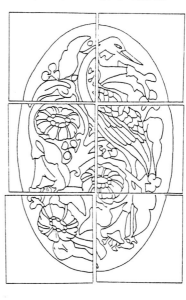

TWO PARROTS OR
"SCARLET MACAWS"

CRESTED CRANE

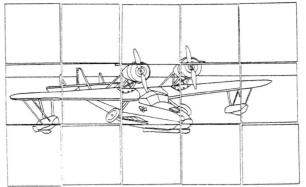

DOUGLAS DOLPHIN —
MR. WRIGLEY CALLED IT
"THE BOAT"

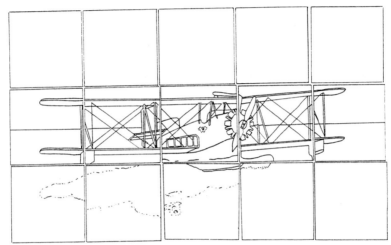

LOENING AMPHIBIAN

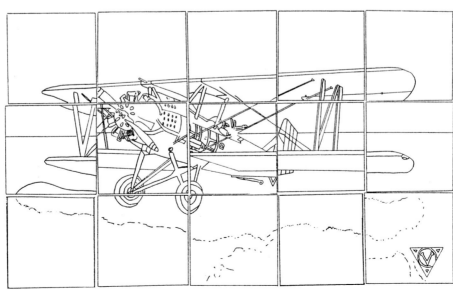

YOUGHT AIRCRAFT
DESIGNED FOR U.S. NAVY

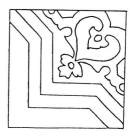

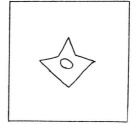

DESERT SCENE — 6 TILES

THE ORIGINAL CASINO TILE IS ONE PIECE IN PATIO
OF D. M. RENTON RESIDENCE — LATER MADE IN SIX
TILES FOR TABLE TOPS

APPENDICES
How the Tiles Were Made

A close affinity exists between the earth and those of us who tread upon it. Instinctively, children are drawn to clay. During play and with no provocation they form functional objects from the "dirt" which, with practice, can become quite sophisticated structures like miniature buildings, roads, even bridges. Reflecting back to prehistoric times it is easy to imagine that the earliest people were forming rough vessels of earthen materials to hold water and food and later creating crude building materials in similar fashion. There remains only a small evolutionary step to decorative tiles as we know them.

Some earthen materials when wet can be shaped readily by hand and the resulting form will maintain its shape without assistance. With the addition of heat either from the sun or from fire the form will harden, thus making it less fragile and potentially useful. However, tile making, like the making of pottery, is problematic; the key is in finding just the right combination of clays, moisture and heat for each product.

Since no technical records remain regarding the making of tiles on Santa Catalina Island, we can only speculate as to how the tiles were made based on what we know of other manufacturers' processes from the same period and what we have learned from examining the Catalina tiles themselves. The facilities were established at Pebbly Beach during the 1920s. The first clay products were strictly functional: bricks, hollow tile for wall construction, drain tiles for waste water and mission tiles for roofs. Clay pavers came later, followed by the famous glazed decoratives that were in production by early 1929.

Raw clays extracted from various locations on the island and transported to the site at Pebbly Beach would first be subjected to grinding and screening before being mixed with water to form a batch suitable for use in making tiles. The bricks, as well as the hollow, drain and mission tiles, were likely formed by an extrusion process in which the clays, properly pre mixed, would be fed into an electrified auger machine that forced it through a dye of the proper shape. Once back in the open air, the extruded clay would be mechanically cut in specified lengths and then allowed to dry before firing.

Due to the warm, semitropical climate of southern California, the clay products could be dried in the open air. A large tunnel dryer in the main building extracted all residual moisture from the clay. The firing occurred in oil-fueled "field kilns" located outside adjacent buildings. It is likely that all of the products requiring only one fire (bricks, hollow, drain, and Mission tiles) were fired here.

It is probable that the Catalina patio tiles were made from a slurry, a liquefied mix poured from large mixing vats through hoses into wooden or plaster molds. The use of molds would have facilitated the manufacture of multiple sized tiles as well as those with incised decoration, both characteristic of the Catalina pavers.

Decorative wall tiles were likely produced in plaster molds as well, but these tiles would likely have been made from "plastic" or malleable clay rather than from a slurry. Plastic clay lends itself to mechanical pressing into precast shapes. To create a relief design on a production tile, for example, a model is first formed in clay or wax from which a plaster mold is made. The design in the hardened plaster mold is recessed, rather than raised. Clay is then mechanically or hand pressed into the mold and when removed exhibits the relief design of the original model. The same mold may be used many times before being replaced.

Unlike the other clay products, the tiles and pottery destined to be glazed would first be bisque fired to a temperature in excess of 2000 degrees Fahrenheit, then decorated with glaze and finally refired. The second firing occurred in one of two periodic, updraft kilns in the factory itself. These kilns were designed to fire intermittently and at a lower temperature specifically suited to the glaze composition. During this fire the tiles would be placed in saggers, clay boxes designed to protect the ware from the various impurities generated within the kiln. The two-fire process made it easier for the glazers and the tile artists to handle the ware during the critical decorative process between firings.

The solid colored tiles were probably hand dipped in liquid glaze prior to the second firing. When more than one glaze was needed on a single tile, it became necessary to insure that the glazes remained separate from one another in the final fire. With no barrier between them, the different glaze colors would flow into one another during the fire, compromising both the intended color and pattern. Therefore, an outline or resist-line composed of an oily manganese mixture would be applied to the tile surface by brush or stencil to keep the glazes apart. The different glaze colors would then be individually applied by brush or syringe to fill the outlined areas. With this technique, a multitude of glaze colors could be used on a single tile, a distinctive characteristic of Catalina decorative tile.

Although much has still to be uncovered regarding Catalina's ceramic production, there remains a most colorful legacy to inspire those who wish to pursue this fascinating part of California's history.

Tile: A Brief History of an Ancient Art

Human beings have always searched for new and better materials with which to build and decorate their homes, public buildings, and places of worship. First there were crude bricks made of clay and straw set in the sun to dry. Soon, brick makers learned to strengthen adobe with fire, initially over an open flame. Potters made clay vessels baked in simple ovens to hold oil, water and precious possessions. Combining their talents, the potter and brick maker reached a milestone by adding decoration to satisfy their artistic souls. Transforming raw clay into useful objects in-

volves a complex and intriguing process. Formed by the decomposition of rock under pressure and by exposure to wind, rain and erosion, clay becomes malleable when wet and will retain its molded form when dry. A clay object so formed becomes even more durable when subjected to heat. Although the object may appear completely dry, it always contains some moisture in its interior, and temperatures must be carefully controlled to prevent shattering during the firing process.

Clay is found with a variety of other naturally occurring materials that when fired create a spectrum of earthy colors ranging from white and light beige to deep reddish brown and even black. Along with the myriad colors, different finished strengths are obtained by adjusting both the components of the clay body and the firing temperatures. Some clays are heavy and coarse, suitable only for bricks, others are fine enough for the most delicate porcelains.

While some scholars have recently dated the beginnings of fired clay to 26,000 B.C., the complicated process of making durable and beautiful glazed tile is nearly 7,000 years old. The earliest decorative tiled walls were found in the Middle East and date to 4,700 B.C. Later the Egyptians developed tiles elegant enough to please the Pharaohs. The Babylonians added to the beauty of their tombs and other buildings by discovering the secret of colored glazes. By 300 B.C., tiles were commonly used for building decoration in China.

The techniques of brick and tile making spread across the continent of Europe. Geometric and natural forms can be found in the ceramics made by the followers of Islam in the Near East and North Africa. Forbidden by their religion to portray the human body in their artwork, they created dazzling designs that decorated their palaces and places of worship. The Moors of northern Africa brought this style with them into Spain in the 8th century. By the 14th century their skill had resulted in the creation of architectural wonders such as the palace of the Alhambra in Granada, the last Moorish stronghold in Spain.

Fifteenth century Florence saw the development of decorative terra cotta (clay) facades and panels, a process which spread as far as England. Church floors of the period were marvels of ornamentation, composed of elaborate tile patterns. During the 17th and 18th centuries, decorative tile was installed nearly everywhere in Europe, from exterior house signs in Italy to the floors, walls, and ceilings of Dutch homes.

With industrialization and the spread of towns in the late 18th and early 19th centuries came the increased need for reliable building materials. The common brick gained new status. Simultaneously, there was a resurgence of interest in the culture of the medieval period. In architecture, terra cotta facades and floor tiles were once again in vogue.

With the rapid growth of cities and towns in the United States, many architectural and design styles were borrowed from Europe. Among the millions of immigrants who came to America before the turn of the century were many workers skilled in the techniques of terra cotta, art pottery and decorative tile work. As the demand for clay materials grew, the need for more efficient means of production was magnified. The factory and not the craftsman became the producer, and efficient production meant that more people had access to ceramic products. But the unique nature of hand-created ware was in danger of being lost.

The craft revival of the late 19th and early 20th centuries in America created a renaissance of interest in the decorative arts. During this period of great imagination and productivity, interest in ancient glazing and manufacturing techniques grew; there was a flowering of new designs and uses in ceramics. Beginning in the early 1920s on California's Santa Catalina Island, businessman William Wrigley, Jr. lent his patronage to a most creative enterprise: the manufacture of distinctive clay products, including decorative tile and art pottery.

BIBLIOGRAPHY

Angle, Paul M. *Philip K. Wrigley: A Memoir of a Modest Man.* Chicago: Rand McNally: 1975.

Anon. "William Wrigley, Jr., American." *Fortune* (April 1932):96–99.

"Bogged Auto Starts New Industry," *Los Angeles Times* (October 9, 1932).

Bowman, Judy. "Catalina's Industry," *The Catalina Explorer* (April 1986).

_____. "Catalina Pottery," *The Catalina Explorer* (May 1986).

Anon. "Catalina Pottery and Tile," *California Art and Architecture* (December 1932).

The Catalina Islander. Anonymous Articles
"D.M. Renton's New Home Sold to Phillip K. Wrigley" (May 4, 1927).
"Catalina Branch Bank Throughly Up-to-Date" (September 10, 1930).
"Catalina Pottery is Now Displayed in Los Angeles" (September 2, 1931).
"Catalina-Made Tables Attract Much Attention" (February 3, 1932).

"Ceramic History," *American Ceramic Society Bulletin,* Vol.22, No.5 (May 15, 1943).

Chipman, Jack. "The Pottery of Catalina Island," *The Antique Trader* (August 5, 1981).

Croom, Henry C. "Arizona Biltmore Restoration," *Flash Point,* Tile Heritage Foundation Newsletter, Healdsburg, California (April–September 1988).

Dietrich, Waldmar Fenn. State of California Division of Mines and Mining. *The Clay Resources and the Ceramic Industry of California,* Bulletin No. 99 (January 1928).

Fridley, A.W. Catalina Pottery: *The Early Years, 1927-1937.* LosAngeles: A.W. Fridley, pb.: 1977.

_____. "Catalina Island Tiles and Tables," *The Glaze* (August 1983).

Garvey, Linda. "John Gabriel Beckman, the Man Behind the Murals," *The Catalina Explorer* (April 1986).

_____. "John Gabriel Beckman," *The Catalina Explorer* (May 1986).

Goodman, Adrianne. "The Jewels of Avalon," *Los Angeles Times* (September 17, 1989).

Hamilton, David. *The Thames and Hudson Manual of Architectural Ceramics.* New York: Thames and Hudson: 1978.

Mallan, Chicki. *Guide to Catalina and California's Channel Islands.* Chico, California: Moon Publications: 1988.

Moore, Patricia Ann. *The Casino: Avalon, California. Avalon, California:* Catalina Island Museum Society, Inc.: 1979.

Overholt, Alma. *The Catalina Islander.*
"Catalina Pottery as an Advertisement of the Magic Isle" (September 14, 1932).
"Catalina Pottery Gaining Buyers Who Seek 'Finds' " (November 25, 1931).
"Catalina Pottery Wins First Place" (March 30, 1932).
"Color to Order: Pottery Reflects our Joyous Moods" (December 21, 1932).

Parmelee, Cullen W. *Ceramic Glazes.* Chicago: Industrial Publications, Inc.: 1948.

Poore, Patricia. "Tile Roofs," *The Old House Journal* (September–October, 1987): 22–29.

Riley, Noel. *Tile Art: A History of Decorative Ceramic Tiles.* Secaucus, N.J.: Chartwell Books: 1987.

Rindge, Ronald L. *Ceramic Art of the Malibu Potteries.* Malibu, California: Malibu Lagoon Museum: 1988.

Rosenthal, Lee. "Bud, This One's For You!" *Flash Point* (April-September 1988).

Taylor, Joseph. "Bill Wyatt: An Official Company Historian," *Flash Point,* Tile Heritage Foundation (January–March 1988).

"Works Progress Administration. Productivity and Employment in Selected Industries," *Brick and Tile.*

Zimmerman, William, Jr., *William Wrigley, Jr.: The Man and His Business 1861 to 1932.* Chicago: Private Printing: 1935.

MANUSCRIPTS AND BROCHURES

Brick and tile equipment lists, December 13, 1938 and January 4, 1939

Catalina Clay Products: Dealers' Price List, September 15, 1931

Catalina Clay Products: Organization Chart, 1932

Catalina Tables. Los Angeles: C.R. Kayser & Company, "Sole Distributors of Catalina Tables"

Catalog and Price List of Catalina Clay Products, Santa Catalina Island, California, 1929

Correspondence: Gladding, McBean to Santa Catalina Island Company, January 23, 1947

Correspondence: Santa Catalina Island Company to Gladding, McBean, March 26, 1938

Correspondence: Santa Catalina Island Company to Gladding, McBean, August 8, 1938

Pottery Suggestions for 1934: Catalinaware From Catalina Island

Santa Catalina Island Company, Clay Products Division-General Price List No.1, January 1, 1934

ORAL HISTORIES
conducted by Lee Rosenthal

Limbeck, Bernice (tile decorator and publicity model), 1991

Limbeck, Earl (machinist, assembled tile table tops), 1991

Lopez, Gloria (pottery finisher), 1988

Renton, Malcolm (ESCI vice president), 1988

Tyler, Dr.John (tile stenciler), 1988

Upton, Roger (Bud) (artist, designer, decorator), 1988

Windle, Johnnie (island transportation), 1988i

FOOTNOTES

[1] Anon. "William Wrigley Jr., American." *Fortune,* April 1932, pp. 96–99

[2] William Zimmerman, Jr. *William Wrigley, Jr.: The Man and His Business,* p.241

[3] Interview with Malcolm Renton, 1988

[4] Interview with Johnnie Windle, 1988

[5] Interview with Malcolm Renton, 1988

[6] Paul M. Angle, *Philip K. Wrigley: Memoir of a Modest Man,* p.55

[7] Interview with Earl Limbeck, 1991

[8] "Catalina Made Tables Attract Much Attention". *The Catalina Islander,* February 2, 1932

[9] Alma Overholt, "Color To Order: Pottery Reflects Our Joyous Moods." *The Catalina Islander,* December 21, 1932

[10] Interview with Bud Upton, 1988

[11] Interview with Gloria Lopez, 1988

[12] Interview with Bernice Limbeck, 1991

[13] "Catalina Pottery and Tile". *California Art and Architecture,* December 1932

[14] Interview with Malcolm Renton, 1988

[15] Gladding, McBean to Santa Catalina Island Company, January 23, 1947

[16] Croom, Henry C. "Arizona Biltmore Restoration." *Flash Point,* Tile Heritage Foundation, April–September 1988